THE SPECTACULAR SCIENCE OF
VEHICLES

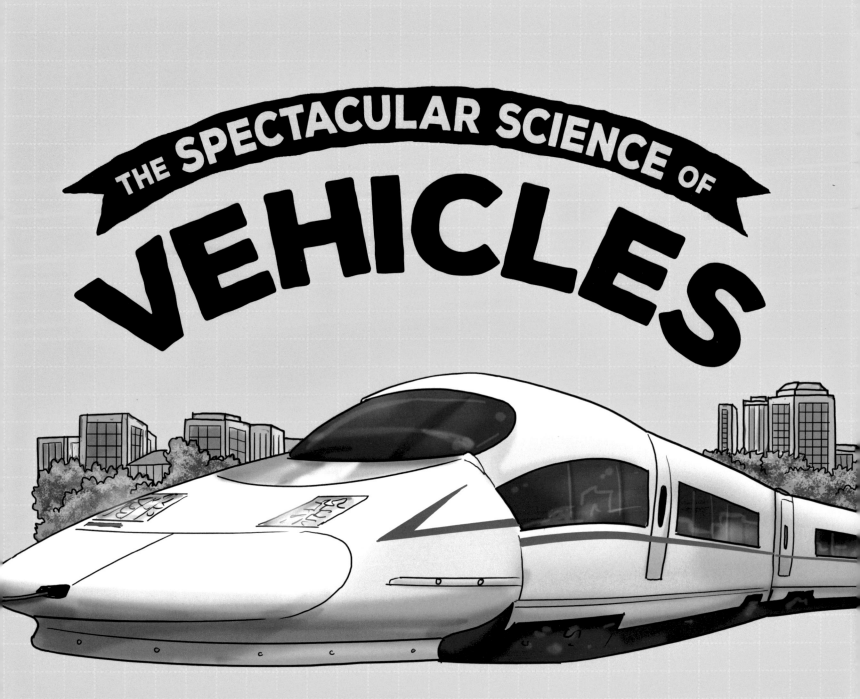

written by Rob Colson

illustrated by
Moreno Chiacchiera

KINGFISHER
LONDON & NEW YORK

KINGFISHER
LONDON & NEW YORK

First published 2024 in the United States
by Kingfisher
120 Broadway, New York, NY 10271
Kingfisher is an imprint of
Macmillan Children's Books, London
All rights reserved.

Copyright © Macmillan Publishers
International Ltd 2024

ISBN 978-0-7534-7967-4

Distributed in the U.S. and Canada by Macmillan,
120 Broadway, New York, NY 10271

Library of Congress Cataloging-in-Publication
data has been applied for.

Author: Rob Colson
Illustrator: Moreno Chiacchiera
Consultant: Penny Johnson
Designed and edited by Tall Tree Ltd

Kingfisher Books are available for special
promotions and premiums.
For details contact:
Special Markets Department, Macmillan
120 Broadway, New York, NY 10271.

For more information please visit:
www.kingfisherbooks.com

Printed in China
2 4 6 8 9 7 5 3 1
1TR/0224/WKT/RV/128MA

EU representative:
1st Floor, The Liffey Trust Centre
117-126 Sheriff Street Upper,
Dublin 1 D01 YC43

CONTENTS

VEHICLES THROUGH TIME

c.8000 BCE
Found in the Netherlands, the oldest known canoe dates from about 10,000 years ago. It was made from a single pine log and was probably used for fishing.

c.3500 BCE
People living in Central Asia domesticated horses and started to ride them.

c.3000 BCE
People began to explore the Pacific Islands, reaching them by catamaran canoes.

2400 BCE
Wheeled chariots pulled by oxen were used as a military weapon in ancient Mesopotamia (modern-day Iraq).

1783
The French Montgolfier brothers demonstrated their new hot air balloon in front of an amazed crowd in Versailles, France.

1981
The first reusable spacecraft, the Space Shuttle Columbia, made its first journey.

2023
SpaceX launched its first test flight of Starship, the most powerful rocket ever made. The rocket is being developed as part of a project to send a manned mission to Mars.

2021
The world's first electric cargo ship, MV *Yara Birkeland*, took to the seas. It is capable of operating fully autonomously without a crew.

2002
The world's first commercial maglev train service, the Shanghai Transrapid, began operation.

1976
Concorde started the first regular supersonic passenger jet service.

1969
NASA's Apollo 11 mission put the first humans on the Moon.

1825

The first public railway service using steam locomotives opened in England. The Stockton and Darlington Railway used locomotives built by engineer George Stephenson (1791–1848).

1807

Built by American inventor Robert Fulton (1765–1815), the first commercial steam-powered paddleboat, *Clermont*, made its maiden voyage on the Hudson River.

1858

The first manned glider, designed by British inventor George Cayley, made its first successful flight, piloted by one of Cayley's employees.

1863

The world's first underground urban railway, the Metropolitan Railway, started service. It ran between Paddington and Farringdon in London.

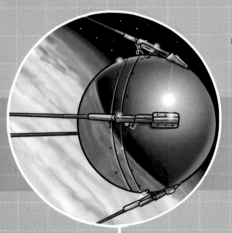

1879

German company Siemens & Halske demonstrated the world's first electric train with a journey across Berlin.

1888

The first gasoline-powered motorcar, the Model 3 Benz, went into production in Germany.

1957

The first satellite, Sputnik 1, was launched into orbit by the Soviet Union.

1939

The German Heinkel He 178, the first jet aircraft, made its first flight.

1933

The first modern passenger airliner, the Boeing 247, entered service. It had room for 10 passengers.

1903

The American Wright brothers made the first powered heavier-than-air flight in their biplane the *Wright Flyer*. The aircraft flew 850 feet on the longest of its four flights.

THE AGE OF SAIL

In the 18th century, large sailing ships called clippers carried goods around the world. These were the fastest ships of their time, capable of covering up to 250 miles in a day.

The ship's carpenter made repairs to damaged masts or damaged parts of the hull. The ship also carried spare sails.

Clippers were operated by a crew of up to 100 sailors. Life at sea was hard. Everybody worked 12 hours every day and often the whole crew had to pitch in to set the sails.

Navigation was the job of the captain and the first mate. They used an instrument called a sextant to determine the ship's position by measuring the angle of the Sun during the day or stars at night.

The ship had a narrow hull to minimize drag and maximize speed.

Each of the three masts was covered with as much sail as possible. The total surface area of the sails was about 30,000 square feet – enough to cover 12 tennis courts.

RECORD-SETTER

The record for the fastest sailing ship ever was set by the US clipper *Sovereign of the Seas* in 1854. It was measured at a speed of 22 knots (25 mph).

It took two men to turn the wheel.

STEAM SHIPS

In the 19th century, new, faster ships were powered by steam engines.

PADDLE STEAMERS

The first boats to be powered by steam were paddle steamers. A steam engine was connected directly to the paddle. The SS *Great Western*, designed in 1837 by Isambard Kingdom Brunel, was the first paddle steamer to regularly cross the Atlantic Ocean. It was fitted with sails to add extra power from the wind, and could cross the ocean in just 15 days, half the time of a sailing ship.

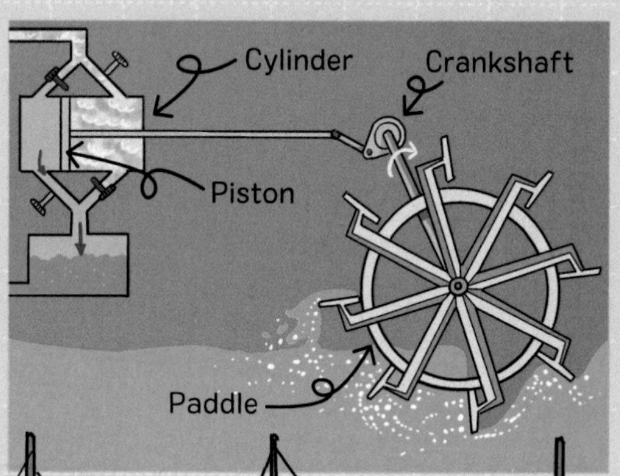

Cylinder

Crankshaft

Piston

Paddle

ISAMBARD KINGDOM BRUNEL

British engineer Isambard Kingdom Brunel (1806–1859) designed a wide range of innovative structures, including railways, bridges, and ships. Six years after designing the *Great Western*, Brunel built the SS *Great Britain*, a ship with an iron hull. It was the first large vessel to be driven by a screw propeller.

TITANIC

By the start of the 20th century, most steam ships were powered by propellers. Huge propeller-driven liners carried thousands of passengers across the oceans. The RMS *Titanic*, then the largest passenger liner ever built, sank on its first voyage in 1912 after hitting an iceberg.

Water was heated for *Titanic*'s huge steam engines by burning coal. More than 6,000 tons of coal were needed for a journey across the Atlantic Ocean. Teams of stokers worked day and night feeding coal into the furnaces in the engine room. The engines turned three propellers at the rear of the ship, which drove the ship forward.

MODERN STEAMERS

Today, many large ships and submarines are powered using turbines, which turn the propeller. The turbines are turned by passing high-pressure steam through them. The steam is made using oil or nuclear power. The largest ship ever built, the supertanker *Seawise Giant*, was powered by two giant steam turbines. It could carry 180 million gallons of oil—enough to fill the tanks of more than 10 million cars!

Seawise Giant was pushed through the water by a single giant propeller. The propeller was 30 feet in diameter and weighed 50 tons. It sat behind a huge 275-ton rudder. The ship had a top speed of 6.5 knots (19 mph). From this speed, it took 6 miles to slow down to a halt.

30 ft

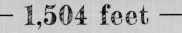
1,504 feet

PEDAL POWER

There are about 1 billion bicycles in the world. In many countries, bicycles are gaining popularity as a cheap way of getting around that also keeps you fit.

Penny-farthing

In the 1870s, the penny-farthing was the first bicycle to gain common use. Its high-wheel design was invented by French mechanic Eugène Meyer. The front wheel was about 5 feet in diameter. The rider sat above the front wheel and powered it with pedals. While the penny-farthing's large front wheel allowed a rider to reach high speeds, there was a long way to fall if they lost their balance, and accidents were common.

In the 1880s, the penny-farthing was replaced by the safety bicycle. With pedals attached to a chain that drives the rear wheel, this is the way bicycles have been made ever since.

Cycling around the world

In September 1895, American adventurer Annie Londonderry (1870–1947) arrived in Chicago at the end of a 12-month journey by bicycle and steam ship that had taken her all the way around the world. Over the course of her adventure, Londonderry had changed her clothing from long skirts to bloomers to allow her freedom of movement. She inspired many other women to wear more practical clothing when cycling.

CHANGING GEARS

On derailleur gear systems, the chain is shifted up or down a cassette of sprockets on the rear wheel by a device called a derailleur. Gears are measured by their gear ratio. This is the difference in size between the front sprocket and the back sprocket. If the front sprocket has 48 teeth and the back sprocket has 12 teeth, the gear ratio is 1:4. One turn of the pedals turns the rear wheel four times. Changing the back gear to a sprocket with 24 teeth gives a gear ratio of 1:2. Now, one turn of the pedals turns the rear wheel twice, but it only takes half the effort to turn the pedals. This is a lower gear you would use to climb hills.

Cassette of sprockets attached to back wheel

Chain

Derailleur

Front sprocket attached to pedals

BICYCLE RACING

The Tour de France is the most famous bicycle race in the world. First held in 1903 as a six-stage race, the Tour now features 21 stages held over 23 days. The stages range from fast time trials held on flat courses to punishing climbs through the mountains.

The main group of riders in a race is known as the peloton. Riders take turns riding at the front of the peloton. With reduced air resistance, riders in the pack use about 30 percent less energy than riders at the front.

VELODROME

Indoor bicycle races are held on purpose-built tracks called velodromes. The tracks have banked corners angled at up to 45 degrees. This allows the riders to take the corners at high speeds. Races can be highly tactical, and riders may climb to the top of a bank to dive down and mount a surprise attack on an opponent ahead.

CARS

Since its invention in the 1880s, the motorcar has become the most popular form of motorized transportation in the world. There are more than 1 billion motor vehicles on the world's roads, including cars, trucks, and buses.

Nikolaus Otto

German engineer Nikolaus Otto (1832–1891) built the first gasoline-powered four-stroke combustion engine in 1876. It provided a practical alternative to the steam engine as a source of power. In 1884, Otto improved on his design by adding an electric ignition, and a year later, fellow German Karl Benz built the first car powered by a gasoline engine. The age of the automobile had arrived.

In 1888, Karl Benz's wife Bertha demonstrated the power of his new car, the Patent Motorwagen, by driving with her two sons 66 miles from Mannheim to Pforzheim in Germany.

FOUR-STROKE ENGINE

A four-stroke engine drives a piston up and down. The piston is attached to a crankshaft, which turns the up-and-down motion of the piston into circular motion to drive the wheels. The four strokes are repeated quickly one after the other, completing a full cycle up to 40 times per second.

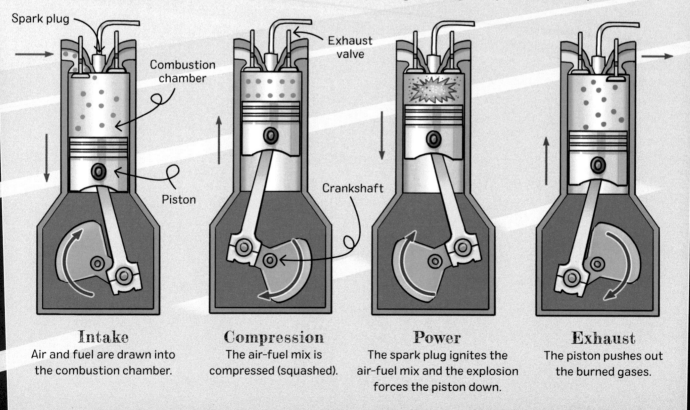

Spark plug

Combustion chamber

Exhaust valve

Piston

Crankshaft

Intake
Air and fuel are drawn into the combustion chamber.

Compression
The air-fuel mix is compressed (squashed).

Power
The spark plug ignites the air-fuel mix and the explosion forces the piston down.

Exhaust
The piston pushes out the burned gases.

THE PEOPLE'S CAR

Mass car ownership started in the 1920s and 30s, replacing horse-drawn carriages. First built in 1938, the Volkswagen Beetle was one of the most popular cars ever made, with sales of more than 20 million over 70 years of production. The Beetle was designed to be an affordable car that could carry a family of four while maintaining a speed of 60 mph.

Unusually for a road car, the Beetle's engine was placed at the rear to allow more space for passengers. This could lead to problems with overheating.

SUPERCARS

Supercars are the fastest road-legal cars. The Bugatti Chiron Super Sport 300+ has a top speed of more than 300 mph. That's faster than an F1 car! Costing more than $3 million, these are vehicles for the super-rich. However, their owners have to take them onto private tracks to test out their full abilities!

TRAINS

A train is a line of carriages pulled by a locomotive along railways. Modern locomotives are powered by electricity or diesel engines, but the first locomotives were powered by steam.

STEAM TRAINS

The first rail networks were built in the 19th century. The crew included a driver and a fireman, whose job it was to tend to the steam engine, keeping the fire fed with coal and topping up the water in the boiler.

SHINKANSEN

The world's first high-speed train network was opened in Japan in 1964. Called the Shinkansen and also known as bullet trains, these electric trains speed along at 200 mph.

The E5 Series Shinkansen trains have 50-foot-long noses. The noses reduce "tunnel boom." This is a loud sound produced at the opposite end of the tunnel when a train enters a narrow tunnel at high speed. The narrow nose allows more air to pass around the train as it enters the tunnel, reducing the boom.

POWERED BY MAGNETISM

Maglev trains glide over tracks called guideways, pushed along at high speeds by powerful electromagnets. They work using the property of magnets that their ends either attract or repel one another.

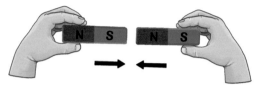

Magnets have a north and a south pole. Opposite poles attract, while like poles repel.

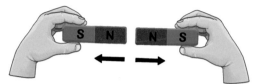

Before it sets off, the train is first made to levitate. A magnetized coil running along the guideway repels magnets on the undercarriage of the train. This makes the train hover a couple of inches above the guideway.

The train is moved forward by a constantly changing magnetic field running through the guideway. As the train hovers above the guideway, there is very little friction to slow it down. In tests, maglev trains have been clocked at 370 mph.

The Shanghai Transrapid maglev is the world's fastest passenger train. It has a top speed of 286 mph and completes the 18-mile journey from Shanghai Pudong Airport to Shanghai city center in less than 8 minutes.

MOTORCYCLES

Motorcycles are a popular form of transportation in places where space is at a premium. Many people also ride them for the fun of it. But motorbikes can be very dangerous and riders need to wear protective gear.

Steam bikes

The first motorized two-wheeled vehicles were powered by steam. In the 1860s, American inventor Sylvester Roper (1823–1896) and French engineer Louis-Guillaume Perreaux (1906–1889) both built motorbikes fitted with small steam engines. Roper later improved his design and reached a top speed of 40 mph riding it. However, motorbikes powered by gasoline engines proved more practical and steam bikes were never commercially successful.

TAKING CORNERS

When taking corners, motorbike riders lean their bikes into the direction of the curve. In MotoGP races, the riders lean at an angle of up to 65 degrees. They wear armored pads on their knees, which often touch the ground.

Speedway riders take corners using a special maneuver called broadsiding. They slide the rear wheel toward the outside of the bend while pointing the front wheel straight ahead.

HEAVY MOPEDS

In some countries, motorbikes are the most popular vehicles of all. In crowded cities, they are cheaper to run and can be parked much more easily than cars. There are more than 5 million motorbike owners in the city of Hanoi, Vietnam. People find ingenious ways to strap goods to the backs of their motorbikes and mopeds.

MEETING UP

On weekends, many motorbike enthusiasts meet up at rallies to share their love of bikes. Every summer, more than 500,000 motorcyclists head for the small town of Sturgis, South Dakota, for the biggest motorcycle rally in the world.

AIRSHIPS

Airships are lighter-than-air aircraft that fly using bags filled with a gas that is much less dense than air. Before passenger jets, airships carried small numbers of rich passengers around the world.

Gondola to carry passengers and crew

HOW DO THEY FLY?

Airships rise up for the same reason that a helium-filled balloon will fly into the air if you let go of it. Helium gas is much less dense than air, so a balloon filled with helium is lighter than the same volume of air. This produces an upward force called lift.

FERDINAND VON ZEPPELIN

German inventor Ferdinand von Zeppelin (1838–1917) designed the first large airships in the 1890s. Zeppelin's designs were built around a rigid frame. Inside, bags were filled with hydrogen gas to provide lift. In 1909, Zeppelin established the world's first airline company and began commercial flights of his airships. These flights were interrupted by World War I, during which the German army used airships for bombing raids over Britain.

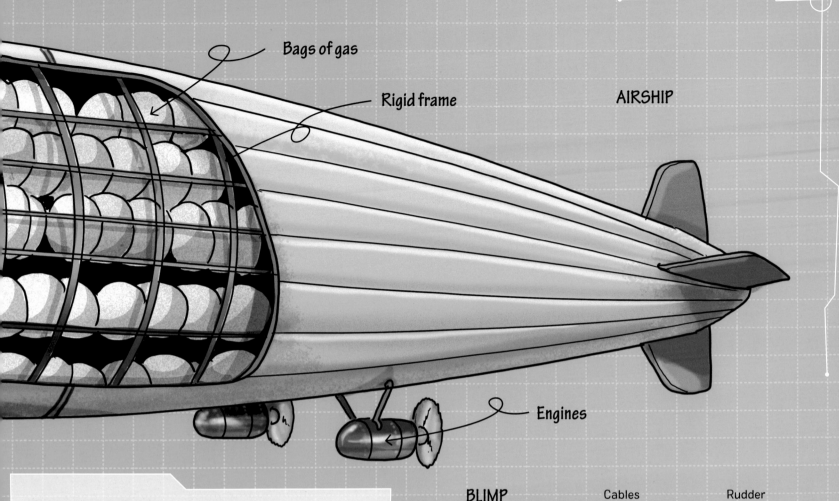

Bags of gas

Rigid frame

AIRSHIP

Engines

BLIMP

Cables

Rudder

Elevator

Outer skin filled
with helium

Gondola

Engine

Tail fin

Disaster strikes!

In 1918, after the end of World War I, commercial airship flights resumed. By the 1930s, airships were making regular flights across the Atlantic Ocean. Rich passengers traveled in luxury on flights that lasted 43 hours—less than half the time of the fastest steam-powered ocean liner. These flights came to an end in 1937, after the German passenger airship LZ 129 *Hindenburg* caught fire during landing, killing 37 people.

Safe gases

The *Hindenburg* burned easily because it used hydrogen as its lifting gas. Hydrogen catches fire very easily when it mixes with air. Today's airships use helium as the lifting gas. Helium is a chemically inert gas, which means that it can never catch fire. The most common form of airship in use today is a blimp. Blimps do not have rigid frames and keep their shape due to pressure from the gas inside them.

NEED FOR SPEED

In the early years of motoring, the fastest vehicles on wheels were electric cars. These were later overtaken by cars with combustion engines, which were then surpassed by cars fitted with turbojets. Technology has been pushed to its limits in the search for greater speed and performance.

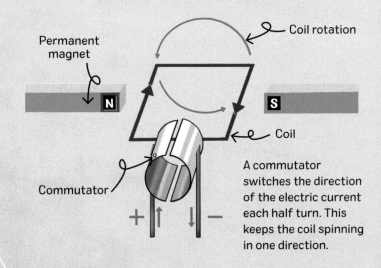

TORPEDO ON WHEELS

In 1899, Belgian racing driver Camille Jenatzy became the first person to break the 62 mph barrier driving his torpedo-shaped car the *Jamais Contente*. The car's rear wheels were powered by a pair of electric motors.

ELECTRIC MOTOR

An electric motor converts electricity into spinning motion using the force of magnetism. An electric current is passed through a metal coil. The current produces a magnetic field around the coil, turning it into an electromagnet. The electromagnet is made to spin by placing it inside a permanent magnet. This is due to the fact that like magnetic poles attract while opposite poles repel (see page 15).

Coil rotation

Permanent magnet

N   S

Coil

Commutator

A commutator switches the direction of the electric current each half turn. This keeps the coil spinning in one direction.

Gas in the fast lane

In 1932, British driver Malcolm Campbell broke the 250 mph speed barrier in his gasoline-fueled car *Blue Bird*. The car was fitted with a huge engine designed for aircraft.

JET CARS TAKE OVER

Since 1963, the land speed record has been held by cars powered by jet engines. In 1997, British pilot Andy Green was behind the wheel of *ThrustSSC* when it became the first car to break the speed of sound, reaching 763 mph.

Thrust SSC was powered by two turbofan engines that were developed originally for fighter jets (see page 26). The engines burned 5 gallons of fuel per second.

RETURN TO ELECTRIC

Today, interest in electric cars has been renewed as car manufacturers look for ways to replace fossil fuels. Extreme E is a series of off-road races for electric SUVs. Teams of drivers compete against each other over multiple stages. They all drive the Spark Odyssey 21, a car designed specifically for Extreme E. The races are held in mountains, deserts, forests, and even across a glacier.

Formula E

Formula E is a series of track races for open-wheel electric cars. Drivers race one another in cars built by Spark Racing Technology. The company conducts research into new technology to combine lighter batteries with more powerful motors and improve performance. The new cars used for the 2023 season had a top speed of 200 mph.

POWERED BY THE SUN

Every two years, solar-powered vehicles race across Australia. Teams use the race to test out their ideas for cleaner, more efficient transportation.

CROSSING A CONTINENT

The cars line up at the start of the race in Darwin on the north coast of Australia. From there, they drive 1,865 miles across the Australian Outback to arrive in Adelaide on the south coast several days later. They stop every night when the sun sets and start again the next morning.

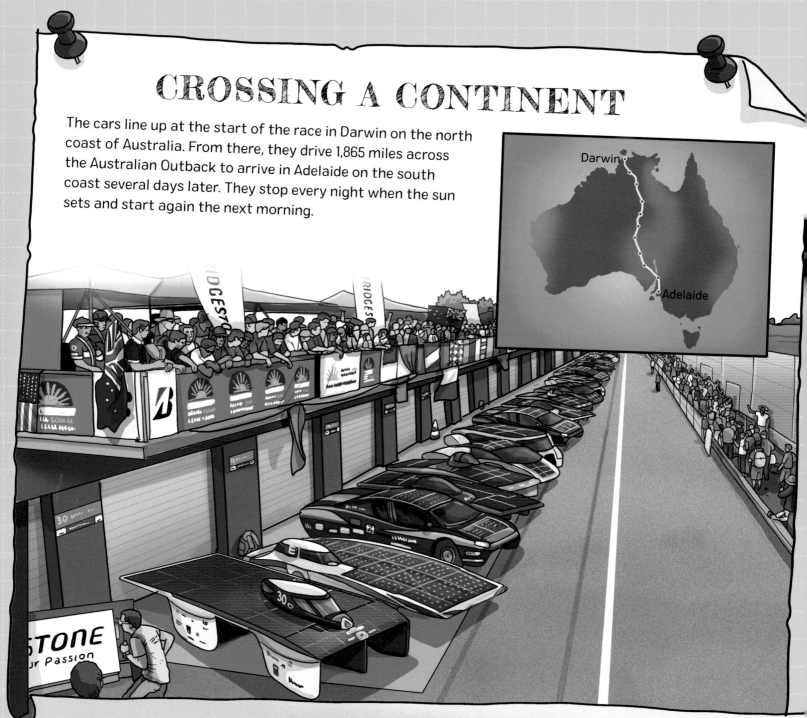

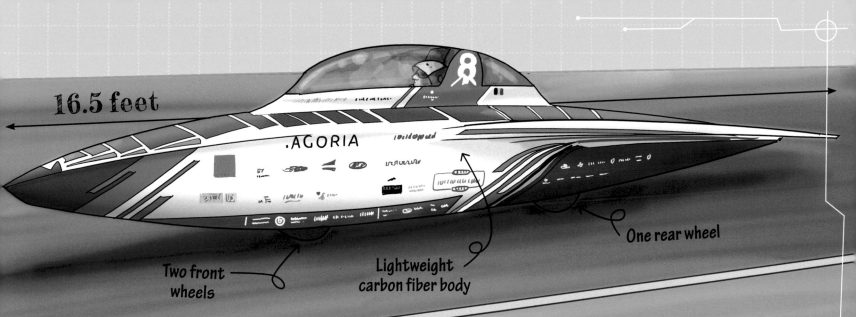

16.5 feet

Two front wheels

Lightweight carbon fiber body

One rear wheel

CRUISER CARS

The race is divided into different classes. In addition to the lightweight vehicles that cross the finishing line first, there is a class for larger "cruiser" cars. These are vehicles that can hold several passengers and could have more practical applications in the future.

Sunswift Racing team members change a tire on their cruiser-class entry *Violet* during the 2019 race. In 2016, the team, based at the University of South Wales, Sydney, created Australia's first-ever road-legal solar-powered car.

LATEST DESIGNS

The fastest vehicles in the race are lightweight and hold just one person. The 2019 race winners were Team Agoria, a group of Dutch engineering students. In 2022, they tested out their latest car, the *BluePoint Atlas* (above). A three-wheeler, it has a bullet design, meaning that its pointed shape makes it as aerodynamic as possible. It is covered in 40 square feet of solar cells. The car has a top speed of 90 mph.

Street car

In 2022, Lightyear 0 was launched as the world's first production solar-powered car. Developed from a design used by Solar Team Eindhoven at the World Solar Challenge, the car is fitted with solar panels and a battery. The battery can be charged from a socket, but the solar panels extend its range between charges, adding 43 extra miles per day for free.

UNIQUE INVENTIONS

Inventors around the world have come up with many novel ideas for helping people to get around, whether they are commuting for work or just messing around with friends in a park.

JET PACKS

Many science fiction writers have imagined superheroes who can fly with the aid of a rocket or jet strapped to their backs. In recent years, inventors have been working on turning the fiction into reality.

In 2008, Swiss inventor Yves Rossy (above) flew over the English Channel strapped to a jet-powered wingpack. He reached a top speed of 120 mph.

UK company Gravity Industries has developed a jet suit with three engines on the back and two on each arm (left). The pilot controls the power with a trigger in their hands and steers by moving their arms. The jet suit is still in development, but intrepid customers can pay for supervised training sessions.

HOVERBOARDS

The self-balancing scooter, or hoverboard, is a form of personal transportation that you step onto. The hoverboard moves in the direction the rider leans into, so to move forward, you lean slightly forward. A device called a gyroscope senses the rider's lean and keeps the hoverboard balanced. A computer controls the power supply to the wheels, which are driven by electric motors.

With a top speed of 10 mph, the Gyroor G-F1 is one of the fastest hoverboards on the market.

E-scooter

The Blitzwheel e-scooter is an electric scooter designed for people who commute to work. When you're not using it, it folds away into a backpack so it can be carried on a train or stored in an office. It has a maximum speed of 12.5 mph and a range of 8 miles.

JUMPING STILTS

Jumping stilts were invented in 2004 by German inventor Alexander Böck. They have given rise to a whole new sport known as powerbocking. The stilts are spring-loaded and allow the wearer to perform jumps up to 5 feet high and make giant strides up to 10 feet long. Athletes wearing jumping stilts have reached running speeds of over 25 mph—as fast as Usain Bolt!

JET AIRCRAFT

Early passenger aircraft were powered by propellers and carried only a handful of people. Today's huge aircraft are powered by jet engines. They can fly much faster than propeller-driven planes and carry hundreds of passengers.

THE TURBOJET

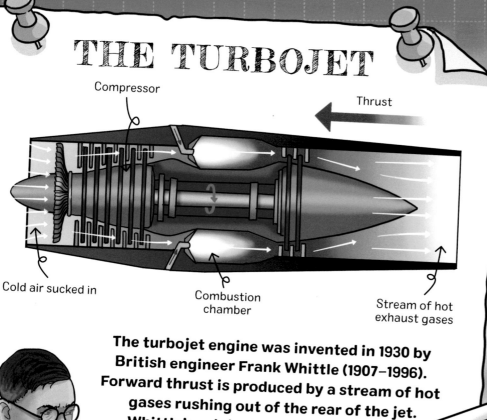

Compressor

Thrust

Cold air sucked in

Combustion chamber

Stream of hot exhaust gases

The turbojet engine was invented in 1930 by British engineer Frank Whittle (1907–1996). Forward thrust is produced by a stream of hot gases rushing out of the rear of the jet. Whittle's original design has since been improved to create the modern turbofan engine, in which a spinning fan adds extra thrust.

A380

GIANT JET

The Airbus A380 is the largest passenger jet in the world, with room inside for up to 853 passengers. On long journeys, passengers flying first class have their own beds!

On the flight deck, the pilot and copilot have access to a wide range of instruments and controls, including eight computer screens. Learning to fly large passenger jets takes a long time. To become a captain on the A380, pilots need to complete 7,000 hours' flying time operating smaller jet aircraft!

The A380 is powered by four huge turbofan engines.

AIRBUS A380

240 feet

Long-haul flyers

The Airbus A350-900ULR has the longest range of any commercial jet. It makes regular nonstop flights from Singapore to New York, a distance of 10,300 miles. The journey takes just under 19 hours.

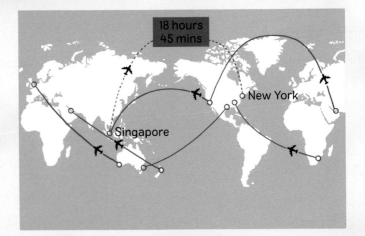

18 hours 45 mins

New York

Singapore

GOING SUPERSONIC

Supersonic jets are aircraft that can fly faster than the speed of sound (767 mph).

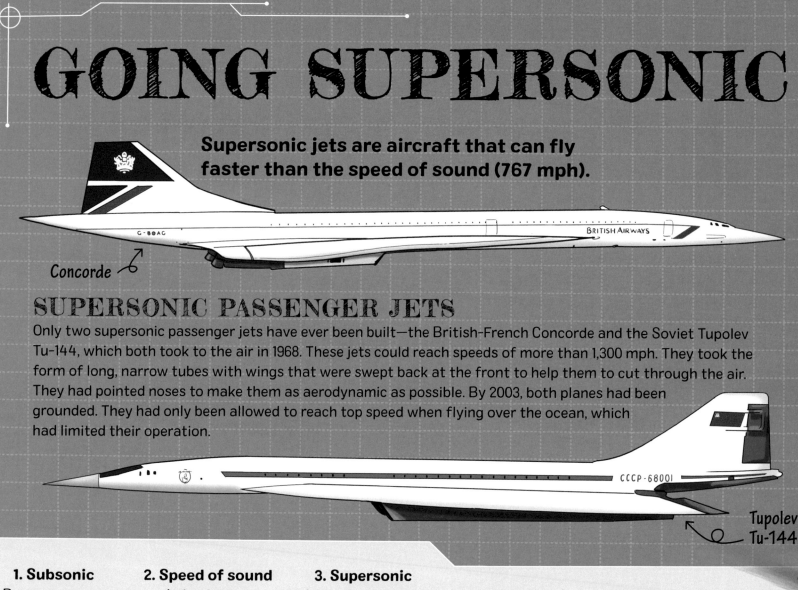

Concorde

SUPERSONIC PASSENGER JETS

Only two supersonic passenger jets have ever been built—the British-French Concorde and the Soviet Tupolev Tu-144, which both took to the air in 1968. These jets could reach speeds of more than 1,300 mph. They took the form of long, narrow tubes with wings that were swept back at the front to help them to cut through the air. They had pointed noses to make them as aerodynamic as possible. By 2003, both planes had been grounded. They had only been allowed to reach top speed when flying over the ocean, which had limited their operation.

Tupolev Tu-144

1. Subsonic
Pressure waves are compressed in front of the aircraft.

2. Speed of sound
A shock wave forms in front of the aircraft.

3. Supersonic
A booming cone of shock waves forms behind the aircraft.

Moisture condenses behind the plane to make it look like it is emerging from a cloud.

SONIC BOOM

Both Concorde and the Tu-144 were banned from flying at supersonic speeds over land. This was due to a very loud sound called a sonic boom. As an aircraft moves, it sends out pressure waves through the air in all directions. These waves travel at the speed of sound. As the aircraft speeds up, the pressure waves in front of the aircraft become compressed. At supersonic speeds, pressure waves build up at the front of the plane and merge into one large shock wave, which booms out behind the plane in a cone shape. By the time the shock wave reaches the ground, the plane has moved on, so you hear the sonic boom a little time after the plane has passed over.

SPY JETS

The fastest jets ever built are military aircraft. The Lockheed SR-71 was made for the US Air Force. Built in 1964, it holds the record for the fastest flight from New York to London, a distance of 3,460 miles. It took just 1 hour 55 minutes. That's nearly an hour quicker than Concorde's fastest time for the same journey.

Built to fly spying missions over enemy territory, the SR-71 was painted a very dark blue color to make it hard to see against the night sky. This led to its nickname "Blackbird."

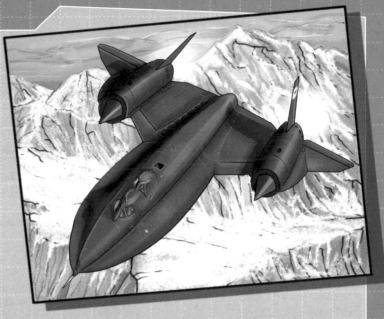

FLYING FASTER

The SR-71 could fly at up to three times the speed of sound. Lockheed is currently testing its replacement, the SR-72, which they hope will fly at six times the speed of sound, making it the fastest aircraft ever. To achieve this speed, it will be fitted with ramjet engines—simple designs with no fan that are often fitted to missiles and only work at very high speeds.

At speeds greater than five times the speed of sound, aircraft become hot enough to melt metal. To resist this heat, the SR-72 will be made from special materials that were developed for the Space Shuttle (see page 41).

TOP SPEEDS OF JET AIRCRAFT

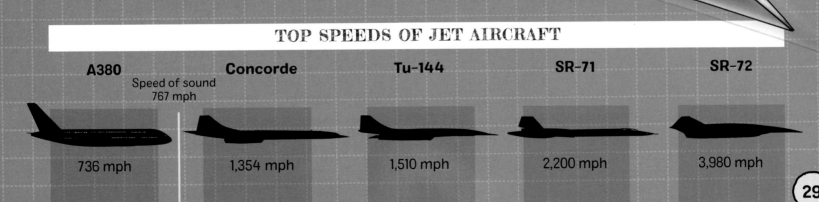

A380	Concorde	Tu-144	SR-71	SR-72
Speed of sound 767 mph				
736 mph	1,354 mph	1,510 mph	2,200 mph	3,980 mph

AIRPORT

Located near the center of the USA, Denver International Airport (DIA) is one of the busiest airports in the world. About 200,000 people pass through every day! More than 30,000 employees ensure that everybody boards the right plane and the planes all take off and land safely.

RUNWAYS

DIA has six runways. Four are parallel to one another, while the other two are at right angles to them. It is easiest for planes to land and take off flying into the wind. To allow for this, runways are chosen depending on the direction of the wind on that day. DIA's runways are about 10 percent longer than the runways at most airports. This is because Denver is one mile above sea level. The air is thinner at high altitudes, which means that planes take longer to take off and to come to a halt when they land. The biggest runway is 16,400 feet long. It is used by large planes such as the Airbus A380.

AIR TRAFFIC CONTROL

Air traffic controllers sit at the top of a tower that gives them a clear view of the whole airport. They have the vital job of keeping track of all the planes in the air and on the ground and making sure that they stay a safe distance from one another. To do this, they monitor the airspace by radar and maintain contact with the pilots by radio.

UNITED

LOADING THE PLANE

Airports have computer systems to keep track of all the people and luggage and make sure they all board the right plane. Checked-in luggage is given a barcode, which the computers read as it is passed along a chain of conveyor belts. The contents are checked by an X-ray machine. Eventually the luggage reaches human handlers, who load it into the plane's hold.

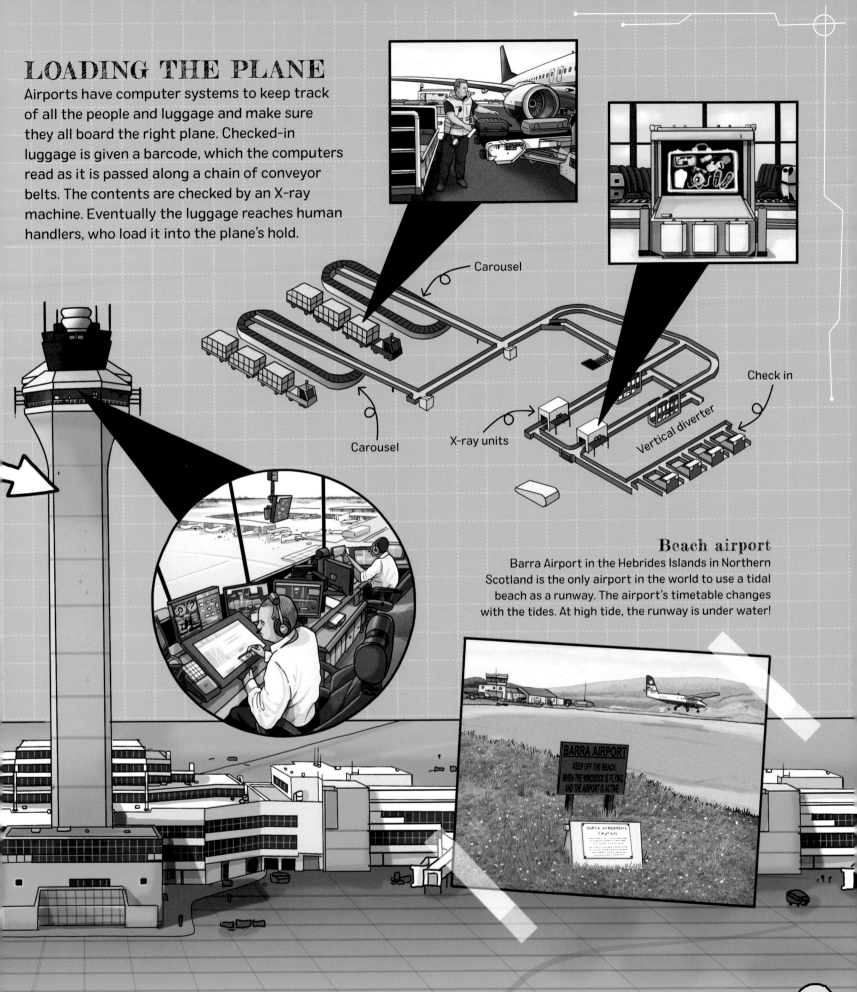

Carousel

Carousel

X-ray units

Vertical diverter

Check in

Beach airport

Barra Airport in the Hebrides Islands in Northern Scotland is the only airport in the world to use a tidal beach as a runway. The airport's timetable changes with the tides. At high tide, the runway is under water!

BARRA AIRPORT
KEEP OFF THE BEACH
WHEN THE WINDSOCK IS FLYING
AND THE AIRPORT IS ACTIVE

HELICOPTERS

Helicopters are aircraft that are kept in the air by a spinning rotor. Able to take off and land vertically, hover on the spot, and even fly backward, helicopters can reach places other aircraft cannot go.

SEARCH AND RESCUE

When people get into trouble in a remote place, such as on a mountain, search and rescue teams use helicopters to reach them. While the helicopter hovers overhead, paramedics are lowered to the ground by a hoist. Injured climbers can be flown straight to a hospital. Mountain rescue teams around the world have saved thousands of lives using helicopters.

HB-ZEF

CHANGING DIRECTION

A helicopter changes direction by altering the angle of its rotors.

Against the spin

As a helicopter's main rotor spins, it creates lift to raise the helicopter into the air. However, it also creates an unwanted turning force called torque. This force pushes the body of the helicopter in the opposite direction to the direction of the rotor's spin. To keep the aircraft stable, a small rotor on the tail spins vertically to create a force that is equal and opposite to the torque.

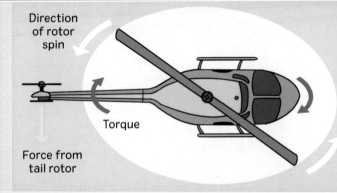

Direction of rotor spin

Torque

Force from tail rotor

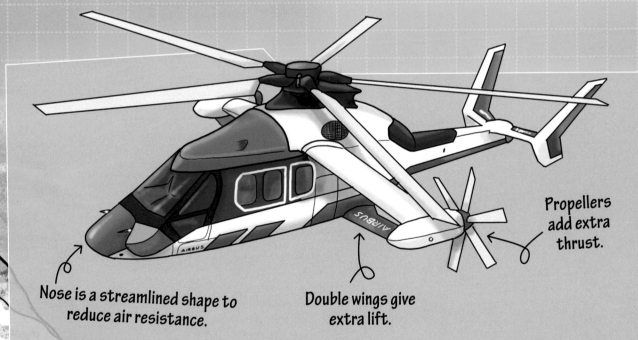

Nose is a streamlined shape to reduce air resistance.

Double wings give extra lift.

Propellers add extra thrust.

HYBRID HELICOPTER

If a helicopter's rotor spins too quickly, the helicopter becomes unstable. This places a speed limit on conventional helicopters of about 150 mph. Airbus Helicopters are testing a new hybrid helicopter called the Racer that can reach speeds of more than 250 mph. It is fitted with short wings and propellers. The propellers add extra forward thrust while also countering the torque from the rotor.

MONSTER VEHICLES

Built to transport goods, rubble, or other vehicles, these are some of the biggest vehicles in the world.

ROAD TRAINS

In large, dry countries such as Australia, trucks often travel long distances across the desert along straight, nearly empty roads. To carry as much as possible, special trucks known as road trains use a powerful engine to pull a row of trailers. Australia's road trains transport freight from the center of the country to ports on the coast.

Nicknamed "The Centipede," the 3B weighs more than 200 tons and is 160 feet long. It carries zinc ore from a mine in the Northern Territory to a port 300 miles away.

MINING MONSTERS

The Belarussian BelAZ 75710 is the biggest truck ever built. It has eight 13-foot-wide wheels and the driver has to climb a ladder to reach the cabin. The truck was built to remove material from surface mines. Fully loaded, it weighs more than 800 tons. That's three times heavier than the heaviest aircraft ever to take to the skies!

Crawler-Transporters

NASA's Crawler-Transporters are two giant vehicles that carry space rockets to the launch pad. Their platforms can carry a weight of more than 9,000 tons, the equivalent of 15 fully loaded A380 aircraft. They were originally built for the Apollo space program in the 1960s, which sent the first humans to the Moon. Crawler-Transporter 2 will be used to transport the Space Launch System for NASA's latest Artemis Moon landing program.

130 feet

115 feet

The longest road train ever to take to the road was a Mack Titan truck. It pulled 113 trailers and was nearly one mile long!

Bendy bus

Measuring more than 100 feet long and with room inside for 256 passengers, the German AutoTram Extra Grand is the world's largest passenger bus. It is bi-articulated, which means that it has two joints that allow it to bend as it changes direction. Even with this ability, it can only be used on routes that don't involve tight corners.

The Centipede has 110 wheels and pulls six trailers.

SUBMARINES

Submarines are ships that can dive underwater to remain hidden from view. Nuclear submarines have been developed for use in warfare. Deep-sea submersibles dive much deeper and are used to carry out scientific research.

New war machine

The first submarine to be used in warfare was a small, one-person craft called the *Turtle*, built by American engineer David Bushnell (1740–1824). It was designed to sneak up on British ships and attach explosives to them during the American Revolutionary War. The pilot powered the submarine by turning a screw at the front, which required a lot of hard work.

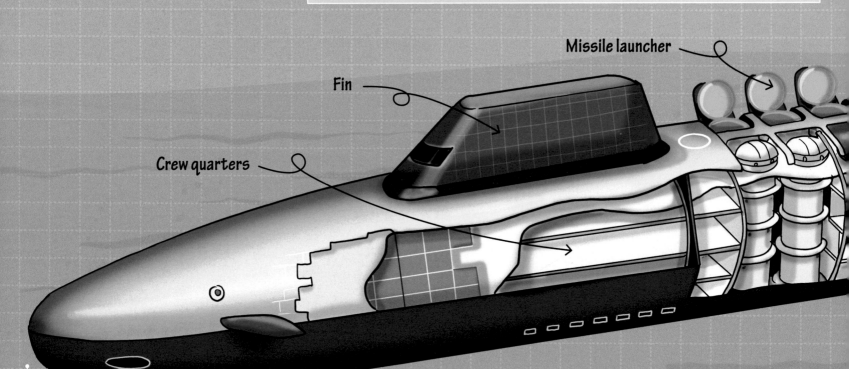

Missile launcher

Fin

Crew quarters

GOING NUCLEAR

The first nuclear submarine, the USS *Nautilus*, took to the sea in 1955. Today, about 150 nuclear submarines patrol the world's oceans as part of some countries' military force. Nuclear submarines are powered by a nuclear reactor. This source of power means that they rarely have to refuel, and they can stay underwater for up to three months at a time.

EXPLORING THE DEEP OCEANS

Deep-sea submersibles carry scientists thousands of feet underwater to study the ocean floor. The submersible DSV *Alvin* has been exploring the deep oceans since 1964. In 1977, scientists onboard *Alvin* discovered a hydrothermal vent on the ocean floor near the Galápagos Islands in the Pacific Ocean. They were amazed to find many kinds of new lifeforms around the vent. This discovery made scientists rethink their ideas about life on Earth. They had previously thought that all life depended on energy from the Sun, but on the ocean floor, life takes its energy from the hot vents instead.

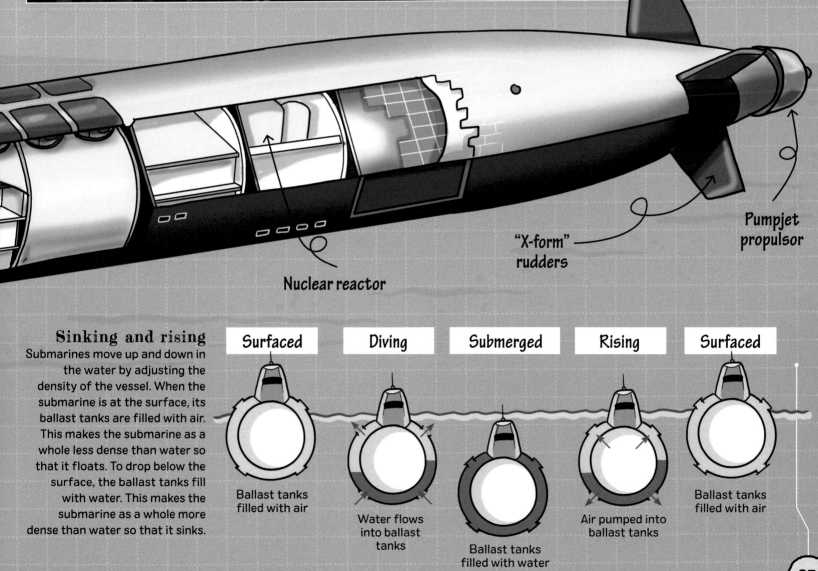

Nuclear reactor

"X-form" rudders

Pumpjet propulsor

Sinking and rising

Submarines move up and down in the water by adjusting the density of the vessel. When the submarine is at the surface, its ballast tanks are filled with air. This makes the submarine as a whole less dense than water so that it floats. To drop below the surface, the ballast tanks fill with water. This makes the submarine as a whole more dense than water so that it sinks.

Surfaced	Diving	Submerged	Rising	Surfaced
Ballast tanks filled with air	Water flows into ballast tanks	Ballast tanks filled with water	Air pumped into ballast tanks	Ballast tanks filled with air

CONTAINER SHIPS

More than 90 percent of the world's international trade is transported by ship. Container ships carry goods in truck-sized containers. The largest container ships can carry tens of thousands of containers.

Containers are metal boxes that are made in standard sizes so that they stack neatly on top of one another. All containers are 8 feet wide. They are either 20 feet long or 40 feet long. The longer containers are the right size to be pulled by a large truck. Ship size is measured by the number of the smaller-sized containers the ship can carry, a unit called a TEU.

The container is lifted onto the ship by a gantry crane.

Containers are kept in stacks until the ship arrives.

Loading in order
A large container ship may deliver goods to many different ports around the world. A computer works out exactly where each container needs to go before it is loaded onto the ship so that it is ready to be lifted off at the correct port. It takes about 24 hours to fully load a large ship. The ships may then spend many weeks at sea. A crossing of the Pacific Ocean takes up to one month.

A special truck called a bomb cart carries containers to the side of the ship.

BLOCKING THE SUEZ CANAL

The 120-mile Suez Canal connects the Mediterranean Sea with the Red Sea. About 50 ships pass through the canal every day, carrying goods between Europe and Asia. In 2021, the *Ever Given*, a 1,300-foot-long container ship, became wedged across the canal, blocking traffic for six days. The ship had been blown off course during a sandstorm and turned sideways. It was finally freed by a team of 14 tugboats, which pulled on the ship while diggers worked to free its trapped hull.

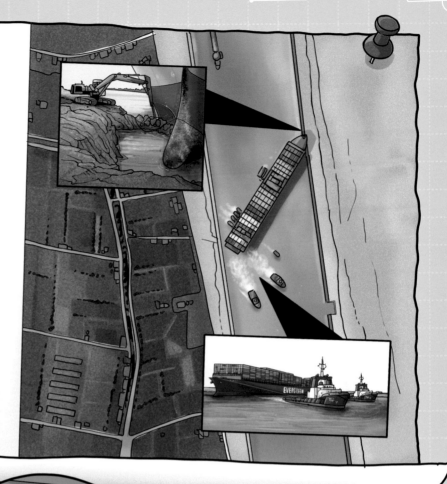

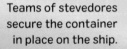

Teams of stevedores secure the container in place on the ship.

Car carrier

Special cargo ships called Pure Car Carriers (PCCs) transport cars across the oceans. The largest PCC, the *Höegh Target*, can transport 8,500 cars, lined up on 14 decks.

SPACE VEHICLES

Falcon 9 Full Thrust is a partly reusable two-stage rocket operated by spacecraft company SpaceX. It transports people, cargo, and satellites into orbit around Earth. The rocket has made more than 200 successful launches since 2015, making it the most reliable launch vehicle ever made.

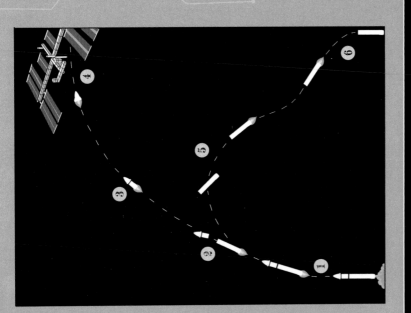

SPACE TAXI

Falcon 9 transports cargo to the International Space Station (ISS). In 2020, its safety record now proven, it was trusted for the first time to carry two astronauts to the ISS.

1. The first stage fires for 180 seconds, lifting the rocket to an altitude of 50 miles.

2. The first stage separates at an altitude of 50 miles. At this point, the second stage fires up.

3. The second stage carries the payload into orbit. Here, it separates from the payload. It will burn up in the atmosphere.

4. The payload continues on to dock with the ISS.

5. The first stage flips for re-entry.

6. The first stage makes a controlled vertical landing on a drone ship in the ocean. It is recovered and reused for further launches.

NINE ENGINES

Falcon 9's reusable first stage is fitted with nine engines. The engines are powered by a combination of kerosene fuel and liquid oxygen. When the fuel is mixed with the oxygen, an explosive chemical reaction releases a stream of gas out of the engines to generate thrust.

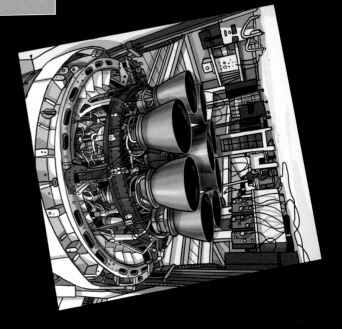

In 2023, SpaceX began testing the Super Heavy first stage for its Starship program. It is the tallest and most powerful rocket ever built. The Super Heavy first stage is powered by 33 engines. On its first test flight on April 20, 2023, the rocket tumbled out of control four minutes after liftoff, and it was destroyed midair. This was the first of a series of test launches. Each test allows their engineers and scientists to improve the design.

SpaceX hopes to send the first humans to Mars on the Starship.

Space tourists

The high cost of space flight means that mass space tourism is still a long way off, but small numbers of lucky tourists can experience space by booking a flight on Virgin Galactic. The 90-minute flight carries passengers to an altitude of 53 miles, where they experience the feeling of weightlessness associated with space before gliding back down to Earth.

Virgin Galactic is launched from the air by a mothership at an altitude of 50,000 feet. At that point, its rockets fire up to carry it to the edge of space.

Space Shuttle

NASA's Space Shuttle was the first partially reusable spacecraft. A fleet of five Space Shuttles flew a total of 135 missions between 1981 and 2011. Two booster rockets helped to launch them into space. They then returned to Earth by gliding through the atmosphere and landing on a runway.

INTERPLANETARY TRAVEL

To send humans to other planets, we need to overcome some big scientific and engineering problems. Scientists at space agencies such as NASA are working on ambitious projects to turn interplanetary travel into a reality. They hope that the first human will be walking on Mars within the next couple of decades.

NUCLEAR ROCKET

To reach Mars, astronauts will need to spend months traveling through space. During the journey, they will be exposed to dangerous levels of radiation from the Sun. To make the trip as fast and safe as possible, NASA proposes building a nuclear-powered rocket. The rocket would be powered by nuclear reactions using the radioactive fuel uranium. This produces much more energy per pound than non-nuclear fuel.

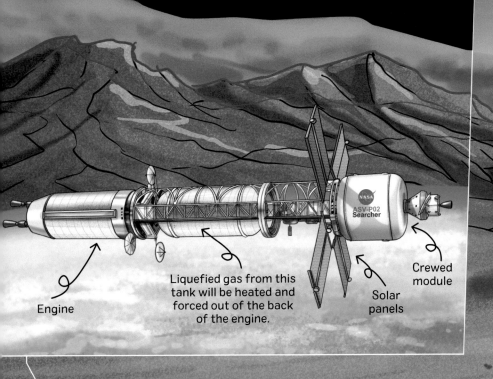

Engine

Liquefied gas from this tank will be heated and forced out of the back of the engine.

Solar panels

Crewed module

MOBILE HOME

Once on Mars, the astronauts will live inside a huge rover that will be both their home and their transportation for the duration of their stay. They will drive the rover on the planet before returning to the rocket, which will return them to Earth. While inside the rover, they will wear normal clothes. When they find something of interest, they will put on space suits and leave the vehicle to walk on the surface.

LASER COMMUNICATION

The astronauts will send back data from Mars, including photographs and videos, using high-powered lasers. This will allow us to follow their adventures from Earth.

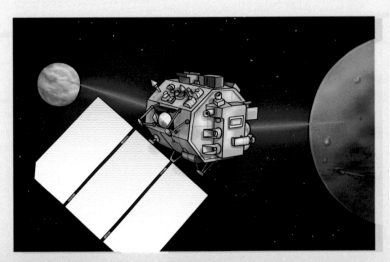

Astronauts will beam information from the surface to a spacecraft orbiting Mars. The spacecraft will aim a laser at a receiving station on Earth.

VEHICLES OF THE FUTURE

The vehicles of the future will be faster and cleaner than the vehicles of today. One day, we may even be sending spacecraft to visit the stars.

FUTURE TRAINS

Hyperloop, or vactrain, is a rail system with maglev trains inside tubes from which the air has been pumped to create a near-vacuum. This reduces air resistance, allowing the trains to move at very high speeds. The idea for a vacuum train has a long history. It was first proposed in 1812 by British inventor George Medhurst. A century later, American rocketeer Robert Goddard proposed sending levitated trains through tubes. Today, several companies are testing new designs that follow Goddard's ideas, and cities around the world could soon be linked up by Hyperloop tubes.

Hyperloop's vacuum tubes could run underground or overground, held up by concrete piers.

FUTURE PLANES

Researchers in the Netherlands are testing plans for a passenger jet shaped like an arrowhead, called the Flying-V. The passengers, cargo, and fuel tanks are all placed in the wings. This improves the plane's aerodynamics, saving fuel on long flights.

ZELEROS

The Planetary Society's Cosmos 1 solar sail

Sailing to the stars

Transportation to the stars is still a long way in the future. The closest star to us, Proxima Centauri, is 4.2 light years away. That's 25 trillion miles, or more than 250,000 times the distance from Earth to the Sun! Reaching the stars requires a vehicle that can travel at huge speeds without needing to carry a lot of fuel. The first spacecraft to reach a star may be a solar sail. Scientists are testing the idea of a giant sail that is accelerated to high speeds by radiation from the Sun. The sail could also be given a push by a laser beam pointed at it from Earth.

GLOSSARY

aerodynamic
Shaped in a way that makes it easier for an object to move through the air by reducing air resistance.

articulated
Having two or more solid sections connected by a flexible joint.

ballast tank
In a ship, a tank that can be filled with water to help to keep the ship stable. In a submarine, filling the ballast tanks with water allows the vessel to dive under the water.

catamaran
A boat with two parallel hulls connected by a frame.

electromagnet
A device made of a magnetic substance with a wire wrapped around it. When electricity is passed through the device, it becomes a temporary magnet.

gantry crane
An overhead crane built on a frame that straddles a workspace. On container ships, gantry cranes allow containers to be loaded in a precise manner.

gears
Toothed wheels that work together to transmit power from one part of a machine to another. Gears can change the direction and power of a force.

hydrothermal vent
A crack in the ocean floor out of which mineral-rich hot water flows.

internal combustion engine
An engine that is powered by burning fuel such as gasoline inside the engine itself.

kerosene
A fuel made from petroleum that is used in jet engines.

laser
A device that creates an intense beam of a single color of light.

lift
A force that pushes up on an object such as an aircraft, raising it into the air.

nuclear reactor
A device that produces a controlled nuclear reaction to provide power.

payload
The useful object carried into space by a rocket. The payload may be a satellite or a vehicle carrying astronauts.

propeller
A device made from spinning blades that powers a ship or an aircraft forward.

radar
A system that uses radio waves to detect the position and shape of objects. The radar system detects the waves as they bounce back off the objects.

sextant
An instrument used to measure the angle between distant objects, such as the angle between the horizon and the Sun.

shock wave
A sudden change in air pressure caused by an object moving faster than the speed of sound.

supersonic
Traveling faster than the speed of sound.

thrust
A force that propels a vehicle forward.

torque
A twisting force produced by a helicopter's spinning rotor.

tugboat
A boat with a powerful engine that pulls large ships.

turbine
A spinning blade that is turned by the flow of a fluid such as steam, water, or air, and uses the energy to produce power.

vacuum
A space that is completely empty of all matter, including air.

INDEX